On Bicycles

SAFETY

K. Carter

The Rourke Press, Inc.
Vero Beach, Florida 32964

PHOTO CREDITS
All photos © Emil Punter/Photovision

ACKNOWLEDGEMENTS:
The author thanks Mike Brackett and Pedal & Spoke, Ltd.
(N. Aurora, IL) for their help in the preparation of this book

Library of Congress Cataloging-in-Publication Data

Carter, Kyle, 1949–
   On bicycles / by Kyle Carter
     p. cm. — (Safety)
   Includes index
   ISBN 1-57103-078-6
   1. Cycling—Safety measures—Juvenile literature.
[1. Bicycles and bicycling—Safety measures 2. Safety]
I. Title II. Series: Carter, Kyle. 1949-   Safety
GV1055.C37   1994
796.6'028'9—dc20   94–20174
                                                                      CIP
                                                                      AC

Printed in the USA

TABLE OF CONTENTS

BICYCLE SAFETY

Riding a bicycle is great fun and exercise. Still, riding a bicycle can be dangerous. Each year many bicycle riders are injured or killed.

As a bicycle rider, you have little protection if an accident happens. Knowing how to ride a bike safely can help you avoid accidents.

Learning how to ride safely can help prevent biking accidents

THE RIGHT BIKE

A bike won't quite fit you like a glove. Your bike can—and should—fit you well.

A good fit is important for safe riding. You should be able to touch your feet to the ground while standing **astride** the bike frame. If you can't do that, the bike is too big.

A big bike is the wrong bike. You are much more likely to fall from a bike that's too big.

Make sure the bike fits!

CHECK IT OUT

If the bike fits, check its condition. The handlebars need to be tight. The seat needs to be tight and set in a comfortable position. The brakes need to work well.

If a tire looks worn or has begun to leak, have it replaced.

Grease and oil keep certain parts of the bike moving smoothly. You can **lubricate**—grease and oil—your own bike after someone shows you how.

*Check hand brakes and
the height of seat*

RULES OF THE ROAD

If you ride a bike on the street, you are part of the traffic. Even as a bicyclist, you must obey traffic rules.

That means you must ride on the right, moving in the same direction as cars and trucks.

You must obey road signs and traffic signals. Be especially careful at **intersections**, the places where one street joins another.

As a bicyclist, you're part of traffic, so you need to ride on the right

An ankle strap will keep loose pant legs clear of the bike chain

Pass on the left when you approach other riders

PLAYING IT SAFE

You can do many things to ride your bike more safely. If you and a friend are riding bikes, always ride in single file. That gives cars more room to pass you. Never ride with two people on a one-seat bike.

Equip your bike with a horn or loud bell. Also, equip your bike or your safety helmet with a rearview mirror.

A rearview mirror lets you keep an eye on the traffic behind you

HELMETS

One of the most important things you can do is wear a safety helmet. A helmet, carefully fit to your head, can help save you from serious injury.

Bicycle helmets are light but strong. In case of an accident, let the helmet take the beating instead of your head!

Always wear a helmet to protect your head from serious injury

USING YOUR HANDS

You need to keep your bike under control at all times. That requires careful and constant attention. It also requires both hands on the handlebars.

If you are making a turn in traffic, however, you need to use your left arm to signal. Be sure that you know how to make the different signals for both right and left turns.

Make a right turn with your left arm raised from the elbow. Make a left turn with your left arm straight out.

This is a left turn signal

BIKE LIGHTS

If you must ride at night or in dim or fading daylight, be sure your bike is well lit!

In darkness you must have a front bike light that can be seen for at least 500 feet. You need a rear red **reflector** light that can be seen 600 feet away. You also need side reflectors on your bike's spokes and reflectors on your bike pedals. Wear white or reflective clothing at night, too.

Bike lights and reflectors are a must in low light

DON'T BE SURPRISED

You can reduce the chance of a surprise problem by not riding too fast for conditions. **Hazards**—things which are dangerous—are much easier to avoid if you have time to stop or swerve around them.

If you approach another biker or a person walking, pass on the left. Do not surprise them! Use your bell or horn, or speak to the person ahead.

Glossary

astride (uh STRIDE) — one leg on each side of something, such as a bike frame

hazards (HAH zerdz) — those things which can be dangerous

intersection (IN ter sehk shun) — any place where two or more streets come together

lubricate (LOOB ruh kate) — to make smooth, slippery

reflector (re FLEHK ter) — a surface off which light bounces or reflects

INDEX